Is Free TV for Federal Candidates Constitutional?

Lillian R. BeVier

T0273231

The AEI Press

Publisher for the American Enterprise Institute

W A S H I N G T O N, D. C.
1998

Distributed to the Trade by National Book Network, 15200 NBN Way, Blue Ridge Summit, PA 17214. To order call toll free 1-800-462-6420 or 1-717-794-3800. For all other inquiries please contact the AEI Press, 1150 Seventeenth Street, N.W., Washington, D.C. 20036 or call 1-800-862-5801.

ISBN 978-0-8447-7113-7
ISBN 0-8447-7113-9

1 3 5 7 9 10 8 6 4 2

THE AEI PRESS
Publisher for the American Enterprise Institute
1150 17th Street, N.W., Washington, D.C. 20036

Is Free TV for Federal Candidates Constitutional?

Lillian R. BeVier

IN THE MONTHS following the 1996 election campaign, calls for "reform" have filled the air. A spate of ambitious new schemes to regulate campaign finance practices have been advanced. Those schemes often include a provision that would require broadcasters to provide free TV time to candidates for federal office. Proponents of free TV bemoan the high cost of political campaigns in general, and of television advertising in particular. They express dismay about negative campaigning; they worry about citizens' losing confidence in the political process and in elected officials; they think that the electorate is hungry for straightforward information and that this hunger can be satisfied by giving candidates opportunities to appear on television in prime time.

. This monograph offers a critique of the free TV proposals. It discusses their constitutionality and their wisdom as policy. The proposals have come in a variety of regulatory packages, all of which are based on a common rationale and pursue common strategies. Thus, the analysis that follows focuses on the following generic conceptual outline of the free TV proposals:

- Broadcasters must donate a certain number of prime-time hours to be used by candidates for federal office during each election cycle.

- Candidates accepting the free time must agree to certain conditions with regard to their use of the time: they must, for example, appear *in person*; or they must directly face the camera; or they must appear for a specified amount of time; or they must agree to limit their own campaign spending or raise money for their campaigns from particular kinds of citizens.

Thus, the essence of free TV proposals consists of two features: broadcasters provide time without being compensated, and the candidates who use it conform their use of it to a prescribed format.

Assessing the constitutionality of proposals with features such as those is far from a straightforward task of doctrinal analysis. Assessing their wisdom as a policy matter is also somewhat an exercise in speculation about imponderables. For, despite having superficial similarities to measures that have been on the books for years,[1] the free TV proposals embody a strategy that differs in kind from anything that has been tried before. A brief road map will help the reader chart a course through the analysis that follows.

As far as the Constitution is concerned, the free TV proposals do not fit perfectly into a single doctrinal category. It is not even obvious whether the First or the Fifth Amendment presents the greater challenge to the proposals' supporters. And with regard to the First Amendment, no one rule provides a complete answer, nor does one methodology chart the obviously correct analytical path. Thus, the constitutional analysis will have something of a two-steps-

---

1. For example, section 315 of the Communications Act of 1934 provides that broadcasters must provide candidates equal opportunities to gain airtime. And section 312(a)(7), held constitutional in CBS *v.* FCC, 453 U.S. 367 (1983), grants candidates the right to purchase airtime at the broadcaster's lowest unit charge. For a brief discussion of the history of political broadcast regulation, *see* THOMAS G. KRATTENMAKER & LUCAS A. POWE, JR., REGULATING BROADCAST PROGRAMMING 66–69 (MIT Press & AEI Press 1994).

forward-one-step-back quality. It will assess the proposals in terms of the several apparently relevant doctrinal categories, noting the aspects of free TV's fundamental regulatory strategy that render so many of the precedents an imperfect fit.

This monograph begins by asking, "Whose Property Is This?" Proponents of broadcast content regulation in general, and of the free TV proposals in particular, gain considerable rhetorical momentum from the explicit claim that "the public" owns the broadcast spectrum. From public ownership, they imply, follows the conclusion that the government's regulatory hand is for all practical purposes free from constitutional constraints: the government as owner is as free as any other owner would be to decide how to use "its" property. First, I critically examine the public ownership assertion, finding it conceptually hollow. Then I evaluate the broadcasters' competing claim that broadcast licensees have the functional equivalent of property rights in their licenses and that the free TV mandates accordingly should be held to be the constitutional equivalent of a taking of those rights for public use, for which compensation should be paid.

Next, I consider the First Amendment issues that are implicated in free TV's attempt to control "Political Speech and the Television Set." The analysis critically examines the current constitutional regime, which entails a different set of First Amendment constraints on the regulation of the broadcast media from those that obtain for the rest of the population, including the print media. In addition, the analysis evaluates the free TV proposals in terms of the precedents conventionally thought to be relevant in the particular context of broadcast regulation. I then analyze the proposals on the assumption that broadcast regulation does not represent a unique First Amendment context. I assume that the First Amendment rights of broadcasters are the same as those of other citizens, and I evaluate free

TV's conformity with the main body of First Amendment jurisprudence.

The monograph then briefly summarizes several prominent free TV proposals. I assess their constitutionality and evaluate their policy agenda. I conclude by expressing the judgment that the proposals are constitutionally problematic, that they would pursue illegitimate aims, that they would in any event be ineffectual, and, most important, that their adoption would run counter to deeply embedded American values.

Whose Property Is This?

An Empty Theme and Its Variations. Broadcast regulator wannabes have found the metaphor of public ownership of the airwaves[2] fertile ground for their claims to regulatory legitimacy. The metaphor of public ownership has yielded a number of variations, each of which comes with its own more or less promising doctrinal apparatus. The "public trust" variation embodies the idea that the *public* is the beneficial owner for whom the licensee acts as *trustee* of the spectrum rights. In the specific First Amendment context, which I shall subsequently consider, there is the "public forum" variation, which embodies the notion that the public remains the owner of the "property" that the broadcast license represents. Finally, there is the "license as conditional grant" theory, which embodies the notion that the government as owner may condition the transfer of "its" property on the grantee's agreement to fulfill certain government-imposed obligations. None of those theories provides convincing support for the regulators' claims. Each nevertheless has sufficient superficial plausibility to warrant examination here.

In evaluating the theories, it is important to keep in

---

2. 47 U.S.C. § 301 (1982).

mind that regulators, politicians, broadcasters, and scholars have become accustomed to the existence of a broadcast content regulatory regime in principle. Two of the most astute and skeptical commentators on the regime have even suggested that "[i]t is too late to argue that the government's claim to own the airwaves is invalid."[3] Accordingly, a skeptic of the regime confronts an exceedingly low threshold of plausibility with respect to arguments proffered in its defense. The regulators' arguments, especially those grounded on public ownership, are like clouds. From a distance they seem solid and impenetrable. Up close they turn out to be no more substantial than dense fog, vaporous yet still capable of hopelessly obscuring one's vision.

Also note that the metaphor of public ownership serves regulators on more fronts than the strictly analytical. In the first place, it serves the significant rhetorical function of suppressing knowledge of what is really going on and changing the nature and content of the debate. As Professor Glen O. Robinson has aptly put it,

> the public ownership claim here is a trope, a way of reifying the government's claim to regulatory authority. The spectrum itself is simply a phenomenon produced by the transmission of electromagnetic energy through space. . . . [T]o say that [the government] owns the "airwaves" is merely to give a property label to its regulatory powers. . . . In common discourse the assertion of ownership is the assertion of a power that demands no further explanation. When it is said that the government (or the individual) can do something with its property because it *owns* it, it is said by way of ending a conversation about the source of power and the reasons for acting.[4]

---

3. KRATTENMAKER & POWE, *supra* note 1, at 227.
4. Glen O. Robinson, *Spectrum Property Law 101*, 41 J.L. & ECON.

In the second place, the public ownership metaphor serves to derail, before they leave the station, the broadcasters' claims that the free TV proposals would amount to a taking of "their" property for which they would be entitled to compensation.[5] The broadcasters' takings claim, constitutionally independent of any First Amendment arguments, is not grounded on the assertion of a right to be editorially free from government *regulation* of content. Rather, the takings claim rests on the assertion that the free TV requirement would constitute a coerced and uncompensated *transfer* from the broadcasters to the candidates of a valuable property right. Thus if the free TV proponents can successfully argue that the broadcasters do not in fact "own" the rights conferred on them by their licenses, they can secure a substantial footing in their effort to discredit the broadcasters' takings claim.

All this having been said, however, it is worthwhile pointing out that the claim of public ownership has been credibly claimed to have been based from its very inception in the Radio Act of 1927 on a deeply misleading picture of the need for regulation. Thomas W. Hazlett, the economist, has argued that in the mid-1920s government officials made and executed a conscious decision to prevent the emergence of a market for broadcast spectrum rights.[6] They desired chaos, and chaos ensued. Congress responded by enacting

---

(forthcoming Oct. 1998) (emphasis in original).

    5. *See, e.g., Spectrum Management Policy: Hearings Before the Subcomm. on Telecommunications, Trade, and Consumer Protection of the House Comm. on Commerce*, 105th Cong., 1st Sess. 46 (1997) (testimony of FCC Chairman Reed E. Hundt) ("[T]he spectrum belongs to the people. Those who characterize public-interest obligations as encroachments on licensees' rights ignore the fact that licensees use precious public property for their own private gain.") [hereinafter *Spectrum Management Policy*].

    6. Thomas W. Hazlett, *The Rationality of U.S. Regulation of the Broadcast Spectrum*, 33 J.L. & ECON. 133 (1990).

the comprehensive regulatory scheme embodied in the 1927 act. If the story Hazlett recounts is correct, notes J. Gregory Sidak, "then Congress in 1927 enacted the most intrusive regulatory controls to that time imposed on the use of spectrum—not in response to genuine market failure, but in response to conscious efforts by the federal government to prevent a market from functioning."[7] The claim of public ownership in the 1927 act was made in the face of longstanding prior use of the spectrum by "homesteaders," some of whom challenged the act as a taking. Although their particular claims lost,[8] the implications of the government's assertion of ownership are on reflection too far-reaching to regard the assertion as anything other than an exercise of political muscle. Contemplate, for example, the outcry that would occur if Congress were to decide that it owns *the air* and proceeded to demand that all communication traveling through the air conform to government regulations.[9]

Public Trustee. In *Red Lion Broadcasting Co., Inc.* v. *FCC*,[10] the Court found significant conceptual support for limiting broadcasters' First Amendment rights in the idea that broadcasters are not the beneficial owners of the rights that their licenses confer upon them. Instead, the public is the beneficial owner: "It is the right of the viewers and listeners, not the right of the broadcasters, which is

---

7. J. GREGORY SIDAK, FOREIGN INVESTMENT IN AMERICAN TELECOMMUNICATIONS 60 (University of Chicago Press 1997).

8. White *v.* Johnson, 282 U.S. 367 (1931); Trinity Methodist Church, South *v.* FRC, 62 F.2d 850 (D.C. Cir. 1932), *cert. denied*, 288 U.S. 599 (1933); City of New York *v.* FRC, 36 F.2d 115 (1929), *cert. denied*, 281 U.S. 729 (1930); United States *v.* Gregg, 5 F. Supp. 848 (S.D. Tex. 1934).

9. *Cf.* SIDAK, *supra* note 7, at 309.

10. 395 U.S. 367 (1969).

paramount."[11] The broadcasters, on that theory, are merely trustees who owe a duty to implement this "right of the public to receive suitable access to social, political, aesthetic, moral, and other ideas and experiences."[12]

The trust imagery packs considerable rhetorical punch. Note, for example, one of its early invocations, in which then D.C. Circuit Judge Warren Burger used it to prop up his court's holding that conferred standing on citizens in Federal Communications Commission proceedings:

> A broadcaster seeks and is granted the free and exclusive use of a limited and valuable part of the public domain; when he accepts that franchise it is burdened by enforceable public obligations. A newspaper can be operated at the whim or caprice of its owners; a broadcast station cannot. After nearly five decades of operation the broadcast industry does not seem to have grasped the simple fact that a broadcast license is a public trust subject to termination for breach of duty.[13]

Advocates of free TV for candidates deploy the public trustee concept to their great rhetorical advantage. In view of the fact that broadcast licenses are extremely valuable and in the past broadcasters have received them at a price of zero, one can perhaps understand the intuitive appeal of the claim that they should be burdened with "enforceable public obligations," somewhat analogous to those owed by a private trustee to the beneficiaries.[14]

---

11. *Red Lion*, 395 U.S. at 390.

12. *Id.*

13. Office of Communication of the United Church of Christ *v.* FCC, 359 F.2d 994, 1003 (D.C. Cir. 1966).

14. Many commentators, politicians, and supporters of free TV have made explicit a supposed connection between the claim that broadcasters have an obligation to provide free TV time to candidates and broadcasters' receipt in April 1997 of a second channel for development of digital tele-

The public trustee concept has superficial plausibility because it draws on a well-developed and relatively familiar body of law that seems precisely designed to provide a cloak of justification for the regulators' plans. The law of trusts permits legal and beneficial ownership to be separated, subjects the legal owner (the trustee) to a fiduciary duty to act solely in the beneficiaries' interest, and penalizes the trustee both for acts that fail to maximize the beneficiaries' interests and for those that feather his own nest. The fiduciary notion appears, as Thomas G. Krattenmaker and Lucas A. Powe, Jr., suggest, to

> fit broadcasting like a glove. Broadcasters were granted a wonderful corpus: "the free and exclusive use of a limited and valuable part of the public domain." The beneficiaries of the trust were the viewers and listeners. They were owed duties. Those would include compliance with applicable laws, but could include more. The broadcaster-trustee was, after all, a fiduciary and therefore was bound to act in the interests of the beneficiaries, even if there were no applicable rules on a specific subject.[15]

On more searching examination, the public trustee concept's plausibility turns out to be illusory, its intuitive appeal unearned. Principally, that is so because the power of the analogy to persuade depends on similarities between broadcasters and private trustees that do not in fact obtain. In the first place, instead of a corpus of property to which a trustee's duty might attach, there is only a metaphor of spectrum ownership. That objection might seem overly formalistic or beside the point: a broadcast license does after

---

vision. *See, e.g.,* Leslie Wayne, *Broadcast Lobby Excels at the Washington Power Game*, N.Y. TIMES, May 5, 1997, at D1.

15. KRATTENMAKER & POWE, *supra* note 1, at 164 (footnote omitted).

all embody a "bundle of rights" and thus has as much claim to be conceived of as a trust corpus as would any intangible property.[16] In the second place, though, the fiduciary duties by which the acts of private trustees are governed are highly elaborated and, while perhaps somewhat indeterminate at the margins, quite clearly specified. There is, moreover, little room for argument about the nature and source of the trustee's duties, about their enforceability, or about who has standing to object to their breach. Attempts to specify—to give concrete meaning to—the nature of broadcasters' fiduciary obligations, by contrast, have been almost completely unsuccessful. The Supreme Court has come up with criteria no more specific than those loosely embodied in the twin assertions that the broadcaster has "obligations to present those views and voices which are representative of his community and which would otherwise, by necessity, be barred from the airwaves"[17] and that the broadcaster's obligations are the correlatives of "the right of the public to receive suitable access to social, political, aesthetic, moral, and other ideas and experiences"[18]— whatever *that* might be in concrete application!

The fact is that, as with the claim of public ownership, the "public trustee" analogy is merely "a trope, a way of reifying [and rhetorically legitimizing] the government's claim to regulatory authority."[19] It was first deployed as a justificatory image at a time when the idea of content regulation "in the public interest" was losing credibility.[20] Though the trustee image has been used sporadically to

---

16. The argument in text, of course, cuts both ways: if licenses are, correctly, understood to convey "bundles of rights," they are the conceptual and functional equivalent of "property" that the free TV mandates would "take" without compensation.
17. *Red Lion*, 395 U.S. at 389.
18. *Id.* at 390.
19. Robinson, *supra* note 4.
20. KRATTENMAKER & POWE, *supra* note 1, at 144–74.

rationalize particular regulatory initiatives, no attempt has
ever been made rigorously or systematically to give it legal
substance or form. Now that the idea of regulation "in the
public interest" seems to have regained favor at least in
some quarters,[21] the public trustee image may well become
merely a makeweight. Substantive legal relationships will
not be affected even if it is dropped altogether from the
repertoire of regulatory justifications, however. The trustee
image never had anything other than rhetorical force any-
way, and it certainly never did any real legal work.

**License as a Conditional Grant of Government
Property.** Former FCC chairman Reed E. Hundt once
asserted, "Broadcasters are given a license to use public
property, and it can be conditioned in exactly the same way
that an apartment lease can be conditioned to say 'no
pets.'"[22] He seemed to be suggesting that because the
government "owns the spectrum," it can license the spectrum on any terms it chooses, regardless of whether the
licensees would be signing away constitutional rights by
agreeing to the government's terms. That straightforward
formulation of a rationale for government-imposed controls
on broadcasting content is not the conversation-stopper that
Mr. Hundt seemed to think it. It relies once again on the
trope of public ownership. But the "conditional grant"

---

21. *Id.* at 174; *see also Spectrum Management Policy, supra* note 5,
at 46. ("The FCC has always had the duty to grant and renew broadcast
licenses only after determining that the public interest will be served.")
(testimony of Reed E. Hundt, former chairman of the FCC).

22. *Quoted in* Paul Taylor, *Fat Cat Broadcasters Should Help Clean
Up Politics*, MAINICHI DAILY NEWS, May 23, 1997, at 2 [hereinafter *Fat
Cat Broadcasters*]. Mr. Hundt was also quoted as saying, with respect to
the free TV proposals: "This is a nonproblematic issue legally. I don't
want to say it's trivial, but it's very close to trivial as a constitutional matter. Airwaves are not private property, and no license has ever been treat-
ed as a private matter." Amy Keller, *FCC Gets Ready To Force Free TV
Issue*, ROLL CALL, Apr. 17, 1997, at 1.

incarnation of the trope brings into play one of the Court's most incoherent doctrines, namely the "unconstitutional conditions" doctrine.[23] Mr. Hundt's assertion begs the broad question of when, how, under what circumstances, and with regard to securing what public objectives the government may, by bargaining with its citizens with respect to government-controlled resources, achieve regulatory purposes that would otherwise be constitutionally unobtainable. Mr. Hundt wants us to infer that the answer to that question is "anytime the government wants, and to achieve any goals it deems worthy," and thus, if the government chooses to mandate free TV as a condition of licensing "its" spectrum, it may certainly do so.

But it is not nearly so easy to resolve the matter in the government's favor. That the government has regulatory power over the spectrum sufficient to legitimize its definition and allocation of use rights has long been settled. That the government has considerable discretion to determine how the use rights should be defined and allocated is also not a proposition in doubt. Nor is there any real question that the government may choose either to give those rights away or to sell them. But those facts tell us nothing about the question in which we are currently interested—which is the question Mr. Hundt's assertion begs—namely, whether the Court would or should hold that the government's

---

23. Kathleen M. Sullivan, *Unconstitutional Conditions*, 102 HARV. L. REV. 1413, 1415 (1989) (unconstitutional conditions doctrine holds that "government may not grant a benefit on the condition that the beneficiary surrender a constitutional right, even if the government may withhold that benefit altogether"); Frederick Schauer, *Too Hard: Unconstitutional Conditions and the Chimera of Constitutional Consistency*, 72 DENV. U. L. REV. 989, 1101–05 (1995) (arguing that, given the diversity of contexts in which courts have invoked it, no single rationale can explain the doctrine); *see also* Richard A. Epstein, *The Supreme Court, 1987 Term—Foreword: Unconstitutional Conditions, State Power, and the Limits of Consent*, 102 HARV. L. REV. 4 (1988).

regulatory power includes the power to require broadcasters to provide free TV time to candidates for federal office. The point of the preceding analysis is that a persuasively affirmative answer to that question does not lie in any variation of the government ownership theme. A more satisfying approach to an answer will require the analyst to specify and scrupulously to evaluate both the broadcasters' claims of freedom from such regulation and the government's claim that free TV for candidates would use a minimum of coercion to implement a genuinely worthy goal. That task is more relevant to First than to Fifth Amendment analysis, and accordingly I shall take it up in connection with the First Amendment discussion.

Who Should Be Paying for This? The "free TV for candidates" rhetoric obscures a central fact: "free TV" is decidedly *not* "TV without cost." To be sure, the proposals to have broadcasters provide TV to candidates would transfer rights without charge, but making the rights "free" to candidates would not make the cost of providing them disappear. It would simply shift that cost from the candidates to the broadcasters, who would suffer an immediate revenue loss that would be reflected in significantly decreased license value. The broadcasters argue that they ought not to be forced to bear the full cost of providing the supposed public benefits that "free TV" would bring. In constitutional terms, they argue that requiring them to provide free TV to political candidates would amount to a taking of their property without compensation.

The Fifth Amendment to the Constitution provides "nor shall private property be taken for public use without just compensation being paid." When improvement of the public condition requires that certain privately held assets be used in particular ways, the amendment requires that the government buy or lease the assets (the "private property") and pay compensation to the former owners. Often, however, the government attempts a kind of end run around the compensation requirement. It attempts to achieve its goal, as in the free TV proposals, not by buying and paying for the use it desires but by regulating or mandating it into (or out of) existence. Often, too, as the free TV mandates would surely do, the regulations imposed for the supposed public welfare substantially reduce the value of the regulated property. When that happens, the private owners claim—as the broadcasters do with respect to the free TV proposals—that the regulations amount to "takings" and that they, the property owners, ought to receive compensation for the diminution in their property's value.

The jurisprudence that the Court has developed in considering those claims is a paradigm of doctrinal unintelligibility. A regulation that "goes too far" is a taking,[24] but the Court has without apology eschewed the effort to articulate with anything like useful specificity the criteria by which it will decide whether a regulation has gone "too far."[25] With respect to the broadcasters' takings claim, however, the free TV proposals may not at first blush appear to present an issue of a regulation "gone too far." That is so because the rhetoric of broadcast regulation has been so insistently (if incoherently) premised on the claim that broadcasters do not really "own" their licenses. Once one acknowledges that broadcasters own—or perhaps it is enough to acknowledge that they have the functional equivalent of property rights in—their licenses, the free TV mandates could not be implemented unless the broadcasters were compensated, since the mandates obviously amount to a coercive transfer, a "taking," of broadcasters' rights.

---

24. Pennsylvania Coal Co. v. Mahon, 260 U.S. 393 (1922).

25. Penn Central Transp. Co. v. City of New York, 438 U.S. 104, 124 (1978) (The "Court, quite simply, has been unable to develop any 'set formula' for determining when 'justice and fairness' require that economic injuries caused by public action be compensated by the government, rather than remain disproportionately concentrated on a few persons.").

Thus, resolution of the broadcasters' takings claim does not appear to require the delicate and complex doctrinal maneuverings involved in determining whether the free TV mandates "go too far." Instead, it requires direct confrontation with the government's assertion that *it* owns the spectrum. As we have seen, the public ownership of the spectrum metaphor provides effective political cover for the assertion of regulatory authority of a scope that the government might otherwise find difficult to justify. In the foregoing discussion of the Fifth Amendment issues raised by free TV, this monograph has argued that the government's assertion of spectrum ownership rests on a foundation both dubious and elusive. Considerable conceptual purchase exists for the argument that, despite the public ownership rhetoric, the broadcasters are owners. Several further points bear on the takings question.

No Finessing the Ownership Issue Where a "Taking" Is the Claim. First, a general point: As I will describe in the discussion of First Amendment issues, the Court has in the past deployed something very like the government ownership of the spectrum argument to justify reducing the level of scrutiny of broadcast regulations. But even if the Court continues to embrace spectrum ownership for First Amendment purposes, it might well be persuaded to take a more realistic view of free TV for purposes of *Fifth Amendment* analysis. That is so because, in principle, the First and Fifth Amendments perform different functions and are designed to guard against different kinds of government overreaching. The Court can vindicate First Amendment principles without tackling the public ownership metaphor head-on, but not so Fifth Amendment principles.

The First Amendment's most important function is to guard against government attempts to control the content of political debate. It appears to be the case that many people do not believe that the kind of control that the FCC has over the years exercised over broadcast content presents a systematically worrisome threat to political freedom. That is so despite the fact that the electronic media are regulated in ways that would be appropriately unthinkable if the print media were involved. Reasons that do not now seem particularly persuasive provided the initial rationale for that system of regulation. The Court has not been eager to dismantle the metaphor of "public ownership of a scarce resource" that supports the regulatory regime. When First Amendment challenges are mounted, though, as we shall see, the Court need not straightforwardly abandon the public ownership metaphor to engage on occasion in heightened scrutiny of regulators' efforts[26] and thus give life to First Amendment principles.

The Fifth Amendment, on the other hand, is designed to prevent unfair and unjust coercive wealth transfers disguised as regulation. The only way that the Court can accomplish that purpose is to hold that a regulation is a taking for which compensation must be paid. Thus, if a significant defect of the free TV mandates is that they coercively transfer wealth from broadcasters to political candidates, then Fifth Amendment principles would be at stake. There would be no way to vindicate them, however, without holding that the broadcasters' *property* had been taken; and there would be no way to reach that conclusion without directly confronting and dispatching the public ownership claim—if not in its entirety, then at least in part.

"The Bitter with the Sweet" Will Not Do. A second general point is that the broadcasters' takings claim gets some support from a line of cases defining *property* in a different Fifth Amendment context. I refer to the line of cases recognizing statutorily created entitlements as "property" for purposes of Fifth Amendment procedural due

---

26. *See, e.g,* FCC *v.* League of Women Voters, 468 U.S. 364 (1984).

process. At one time, the Supreme Court held that individuals who received public benefits, such as public employment or welfare, had no right to procedural protections on termination of their claims.[27] In *Goldberg* v. *Kelly,*[28] the Court reversed that doctrine and held that a welfare recipient's interest in continued receipt of welfare benefits was a "statutory entitlement" amounting to "property" within the Due Process Clause, and thus that it could not be terminated without a hearing.

With respect to public employees, the Court flirted with a doctrine that permitted states to evade *Goldberg* by statutorily limiting the procedures to be employed in determining whether their employment should be terminated:

> [W]here the grant of a substantive right is inextricably intertwined with the limitations on the procedures which are to be employed in determining that right, a litigant in the position of appellee must take the bitter with the sweet.[29]

The Court ended this flirtation in *Cleveland Board of Education* v. *Loudermill,*[30] when it unequivocally held:

> "Property" cannot be defined by the procedures provided for its deprivation any more than can life or liberty. The right to due process "is conferred, not by legislative grace, but by constitutional guarantee. While the legislature may elect not to confer a property interest in [public] employment, it may not constitutionally authorize the deprivation of

---

27. *See, e.g.,* Bailey v. Richardson, 182 F.2d 46 (D.C. Cir. 1950), *aff'd by an equally divided Court,* 341 U.S. 918 (1951) (no hearing required for employee dismissed from government employment).

28. 397 U.S. 254 (1970).

29. Arnett v. Kennedy, 416 U.S. 134, 153–54 (1974).

30. 470 U.S. 532 (1985).

such an interest, once conferred, without appropriate procedural safeguards."[31]

Those procedural due process cases are relevant to the broadcasters' takings claim because an implicit "bitter with the sweet" argument has consistently sustained the government's assertion that its substantially restrained regulatory authority over the behavior of broadcast licensees is essentially unconstrained by Fifth Amendment limitations. Proponents of regulation repeatedly point out that licensees have gotten a "sweet" deal, since they have received very profitable licenses at a price of zero. But the fact that the government has chosen an allocation method that gives licensees a sweet deal does not necessarily justify it in making regulatory decisions that are unreviewably bitter. The procedural due process cases suggest at the very least that the Court might find it intolerable "that the government should wield [such a] degree of potentially arbitrary power."[32] If so, the Court would have an opportunity to conclude that, for purposes of takings analysis, the "property" taken by the free TV mandates is that of the broadcasters, and compensation must be paid.

The Economic Realities of Broadcast Licenses Should Count for *Something.* The Court might conclude, with Thomas G. Krattenmaker and Lucas A. Powe, Jr., that though the empirical premises are weak and the logic flawed, "it is too late to argue that the government's claim to own the airwaves is invalid."[33] Contrary, perhaps, to conventional wisdom, such a conclusion would hardly support the broadcasters' takings claim. The reason is that

---

31. *Id.* at 541 (quoting Arnett *v.* Kennedy, 416 U.S. 134, 167 (1974)) (Powell, J. concurring in part and concurring in result in part).

32. Richard B. Stewart, *The Reformation of American Administrative Law*, 88 HARV. L. REV. 1667, 1717–18 (1975).

33. KRATTENMAKER & POWE, *supra* note 1, at 227.

it would not speak at all to what is in fact the gravamen of that claim, namely the nature of the broadcasters' rights *during the term of their licenses*. Consider that complying with the free TV mandates would require broadcasters to forgo substantial income—as much as $500 million per two-year election cycle—from sales of broadcast time during the license term. The government has never contended that the *income* generated during the license term constitutes government property, nor has it ever questioned the legitimacy of the broadcasters' claims of entitlement to the income.

For their duration, broadcast licenses grant to licensees the functional equivalent of property rights: exclusive entitlement to and prohibition of interlopers from trespassing on their particular spectrum space. The sanctions to which licensees are subject if they broadcast outside the wavelengths covered by their licenses serve much the same function as fences around the borders of real property: they prevent encroachment upon assets to which the law grants others exclusive possession. Another fact indicating that licenses are the functional equivalent of property is that, despite being limited in duration, they are traded in an active market where prices clearly reflect buyers' expectations of uninterrupted long-term enjoyment. Moreover, of fundamental significance to the takings analysis is the fact that broadcasters' expectations of uninterrupted income streams are *investment-backed* and that broadcasters' investment in reliance on the continuation of the licensing regime is encouraged by a number of explicit FCC policies.[34] Regulations that disappoint distinct investment-backed expectations have long aroused the Court's most intense suspicion, particularly when the expectations have been formed and the investments made in explicit response

---

34. *E.g.*, Central Fla. Enterprises, Inc. *v.* FCC, 683 F.2d 503, 507 (D.C. Cir. 1982).

to and reliance upon government policies designed to encourage them.[35]

The more one contemplates the decline in the value of the licensees' discounted net revenue stream that complying with free TV mandates would cause, and the more one ponders the coercive reality of the wealth transfer that free TV would represent, the easier it is to penetrate the smokescreen of the public ownership trope. Hypothetical analogies help too. Suppose that the government leased a government building, of which it was clearly the owner, to tenant *A*. Suppose further that the lease itself said nothing about the government's retaining a right to reenter and claim even a temporary right of possession on behalf of tenant *B* (or anyone else). Suppose further that the government, during the term of the lease, mandated that tenant *A* surrender possession of a certain amount of its "prime rental time" (and concomitantly required tenant *A* to forfeit altogether the income that the right to possession would generate during that time) to tenant *B*. Suppose further that, in justifying its mandate that tenant *A* surrender temporary possession to tenant *B*, the government referred simply to the fact that it "owned the building" (implying that, despite the lease, the government could do whatever it wanted with the right to possession) and then went on to tout the great public benefits that "free occupancy by tenant

---

35. Penn Central Transp. Co. *v.* City of New York, 438 U.S. 104, 124 (1978) (Among the several factors of particular significance in determining whether a taking has occurred is "the extent to which the regulation has interfered with distinct investment-backed expectations."); Kaiser Aetna *v.* United States, 444 U.S. 164 (1979); *see also* J. GREGORY SIDAK & DANIEL F. SPULBER, DEREGULATORY TAKINGS AND THE REGULATORY CONTRACT: THE COMPETITIVE TRANSFORMATION OF NETWORK INDUSTRIES IN THE UNITED STATES 219–26 (Cambridge University Press 1997); Frank Michelman, *Property, Utility, and Fairness: Comments on the Ethical Foundations of "Just Compensation" Law*, 80 HARV. L. REV. 1165, 1223 (compensation should be required when claimant is deprived of "distinctly perceived, sharply crystallized investment-backed expectations").

B" would secure. Can anyone doubt that such behavior would be held to be a taking and that tenant *A* would be entitled to compensation? By a parity of reasoning, *at least as to licenses in effect at the time the free TV mandates were imposed,* the mandates would be a taking and the broadcasters entitled to compensation—even if the Court were to continue to embrace the public ownership metaphor.

Political Speech and the Television Set

A Different First Amendment for Broadcasters? "It is well settled that the First Amendment has a special meaning in the broadcast context."[36] Since *Red Lion Broadcasting Co., Inc.* v. *FCC*[37] was the case in which that First Amendment anomaly became well settled,[38] and since the free TV proposals are aimed directly at broadcasters, *Red Lion* is the most obvious starting point for our First Amendment analysis.

Red Lion. In *Red Lion*, the Supreme Court sustained both the FCC-promulgated fairness doctrine[39] and the

---

36. FCC *v.* Pacifica Foundation, 438 U.S. 726, 741–42 n.17 (1978).

37. 395 U.S. 367 (1969).

38. *Red Lion* was not the first case in which the First Amendment was given special meaning as applied to broadcasters. *See, e.g.*, NBC *v.* United States, 319 U.S. 192 (1943) (sustaining Chain Broadcasting rules against First Amendment challenge). It was, however, the first case in which the Court "enthusiastically embraced the concept of [broadcasting] regulation. It took the affirmative and reconceived the fundamental theoretical underpinnings . . . of the relationship between the press and government." LEE BOLLINGER, IMAGES OF A FREE PRESS 72 (University of Chicago Press 1991).

39. The fairness doctrine "imposed on radio and television broadcasters the requirement that discussion of public issues be presented on broadcast stations, and that each side of those issues must be given fair coverage." *Red Lion*, 395 U.S. at 369. In 1987, the FCC repealed the doctrine,

personal attack and political editorial regulations that the FCC issued pursuant to that doctrine.[40] The Court held that the commission had not exceeded its statutory authority and, more important for purposes of the present analysis, that the regulations "enhance[d] rather than abridge[d] the freedoms of speech and press"[41] and so did not violate the First Amendment.[42]

The broadcasters who challenged the regulations at issue in *Red Lion* made conventional First Amendment arguments that would in any other context—particularly in the context of a similar regulation of the print media—have easily carried the day.[43] Their claim was that

---

Complaint of Syracuse Peace Council, Memorandum Opinion and Order, 2 F.C.C. Rcd. 5043 (1987); the District of Columbia Circuit Court sustained the repeal, Syracuse Peace Council *v.* FCC, 867 F.2d 654 (D.C. Cir. 1989); and the Supreme Court denied certiorari, 493 U.S. 1019 (1990).

40. The personal attack rules required broadcasters to provide an opportunity to respond to a person whose "honesty, character, integrity or like personal qualities" were attacked during a presentation of views on a controversial issue of public importance; the political editorial rule required broadcasters who endorsed a candidate to offer reasonable opportunity for the candidate's opponent(s) to respond. *Red Lion,* 395 U.S. at 373–74.

41. *Id.* at 375.

42. Notice a fact that the Court in *Red Lion* failed to acknowledge: the idea that freedom can be *enhanced* by regulation is in significant and probably irreconcilable tension with the otherwise prevailing view that the First Amendment guarantees freedom *from* the exercise of governmental power. For a brief and useful historical analysis of *Red Lion*'s "enhancement theory," see Lucas A. Powe, Jr., *Mass Speech and the Newer First Amendment,* 1982 SUP. CT. REV. 243, 243–69; *see also* text accompanying notes 72–73, *infra.*

43. *Cf., e.g.,* Miami Herald Publishing Co. *v.* Tornillo, 418 U.S. 241 (1974) (invalidating a state law granting a right of reply to candidates attacked by a newspaper); New York Times Co. *v.* Sullivan, 376 U.S. 254 (1964) (holding that a public official cannot recover damages from a newspaper for false statements made in reference to his official conduct unless the false statement was made with "actual malice," that is, knowl-

[n]o man may be prevented from saying or publishing what he thinks, or from refusing in his speech or other utterances to give equal weight to the views of his opponents. This right, they [said], applies equally to broadcasters.[44]

The Court, however, unanimously decided that broadcasters' First Amendment rights were attenuated because broadcasting was different from other media. "[B]roadcast frequencies constitute[ ] a *scarce resource* whose use [can] be regulated and rationalized only by the Government."[45] Since there is no such thing as a *non*scarce resource, the Court must have believed that there was something unique about broadcast frequencies,[46] a peculiarity that rendered conventional market allocation mechanisms inapt and eliminated traditional First Amendment barriers to government control of content.[47] The following quotations from Justice White's opinion will help the reader to comprehend the Court's mind-set.

* The government constitutionally may license broadcasters to use the spectrum. "Licenses to broadcast do not

edge of falsity or reckless disregard of the truth).

44. *Red Lion*, 395 U.S. at 386.

45. *Id.* at 376 (emphasis added).

46. *See* Turner Broadcasting Sys. *v.* FCC, 512 U.S. 622, 637 (1994) (*Turner I*) (observing that the Court's "distinct approach to broadcast regulation rests upon the unique physical limitations of the broadcast medium").

47. The Court has never specified or explained what it thinks constitutes the "unique" characteristic of broadcast frequency scarcity. Commentators have considered, and rejected, numerous possibilities. *See generally* Jonathan Weinberg, *Broadcasting and Speech*, 81 CALIF. L. REV. 1101 (1993); Matthew L. Spitzer, *The Constitutionality of Licensing Broadcasters*, 64 N.Y.U. L. REV. 990 (1989). For now it is enough to note that *Red Lion* rests on the premise that broadcasting is "different" from other media and that the source of that perceived difference is the "unique scarcity" of the spectrum.

confer ownership of designated frequencies, but only the temporary privilege of using them."[48]

- "No one has a First Amendment right to a license [and] as far as the First Amendment is concerned those who are licensed stand no better than those to whom licenses are refused."[49]

- "There is nothing in the First Amendment which prevents the Government from requiring a licensee to share his frequency with others and to conduct himself as a proxy or fiduciary with obligations to present those views and voices which are representative of his community and which would otherwise, by necessity, be barred from the airwaves."[50]

- Finally, "it is the right of the viewers and listeners, not the right of the broadcasters, which is paramount."[51]

From the time of its first articulation, critics have challenged the "scarcity" rationale that was so fundamental to the Court's thinking in *Red Lion*. They have disputed its empirical premises, the logic of the conclusions it generated, and the validity of the constitutional principle it endorsed. The Court in turn has acknowledged the criticism but so far has "declined to question [the rationale's] continuing validity as support for [its] broadcast jurisprudence."[52] The justices have not been presented with the kind of direct challenge to subsequent FCC (or congressional) regulations premised on scarcity that would have required the Court to

---

48. 395 U.S. at 394.
49. *Id*. at 389.
50. *Id*.
51. *Id*. at 390.
52. *Turner I*, 512 U.S. at 638.

confront the question. But if any of the free TV proposals were to be adopted by Congress or promulgated by the FCC on its own authority, they surely would provide an opportunity to mount such a challenge.

Since *Red Lion* has not been overruled, it must be considered to announce the First Amendment framework governing regulations of broadcast content. Its conceptual and empirical underpinnings are so vulnerable, however, that it must be regarded as unstable and thus not necessarily "good law." Accordingly, with respect to *Red Lion*, a study such as this must perform two tasks. First, it must apply *Red Lion* and its progeny to the proposals at issue, giving consideration to the very real possibility that even if *Red Lion* does continue to provide the governing analytical framework, the case does not necessarily authorize free TV mandates. Second, the study must summarize and assess "scarcity," the conceptual and empirical premise on which *Red Lion* was based. I begin with the second task.

On close scrutiny, scarcity reveals itself as a loosely defined concept whose denotation depends on the particular regulatory agenda that it is deployed to support. On even closer scrutiny, it does not support the broad proposition for which it is most commonly advanced, for whatever the meaning of the statement that "broadcast frequencies are scarce," it does not justify applying a more lenient First Amendment standard to broadcasters than is applied to newspaper publishers.[53]

Scarcity is sometimes used as a technological concept denoting the fact that if everyone broadcasts on the same frequency, none will be heard.[54] The implication of the

---

53. Telecommunications Research & Action Ctr. *v.* FCC, 801 F.2d 501, 508, *reh'g denied*, 806 F.2d 1115 (D.C. Cir. 1986), *cert. denied*, 482 U.S. 919 (1987) (Bork, J.) ("[T]he attempt to use a universal fact [physical scarcity] as a distinguishing principle necessarily leads to analytical confusion.").

54. KRATTENMAKER & POWE, *supra* note 1, at 206.

observation is that government must devise some method to alleviate interference, as indeed it must. But that method need not include government management of broadcast content. All that is required is a method for allocating and enforcing rights in spectrum space.[55] The Court in *Red Lion* seemed to think that Congress had to eschew allocating spectrum frequencies with genuine property rights in favor of government licensing based on an ill-defined "public trustee" notion.[56] In truth, however, once one realizes that property rights are nothing more than legally enforceable claims to exclusive use, possession, and control of resources, one recognizes that there is no technological impediment to using property rights to prevent interference with spectrum allocations. Indeed, as my foregoing analysis makes clear, the present regulatory regime grants licensees rights that are functionally equivalent to property rights.

Another meaning of "scarcity" as a unique characteristic of the broadcast spectrum is that the spectrum is finite: whereas more trees can be grown, more spectrum cannot be created. That is an accurate statement, but it is incomplete and cannot carry the "spectrum is *uniquely* scarce" argument: although more spectrum cannot be created, additional frequencies have in the past and continue to become available as technology improves.[57]

A third possible denotation of spectrum "scarcity" is that there are fewer frequencies than there are people who want them. That too is an accurate but incomplete statement. The distinction it implicitly draws between pub-

---

55. *See* Time Warner Entertainment Co. *v.* FCC, 105 F.3d 723, 725 (D.C. Cir. 1997) (Williams, J., dissenting from the denial of rehearing *en banc*) ("Alleviation of interference does not necessitate government content management; it requires, as do most problems of efficient use of resources, a system for allocation and protection of exclusive property rights.").

56. *See* text accompanying notes 36–45, *supra.*

57. KRATTENMAKER & POWE, *supra* note 1, at 208.

lishers and broadcasters, for example, is the product of a government-inflicted wound rather than an artifact of any natural, unique attribute of the spectrum.[58] The reason excess demand for publishing rights does not exist is that the price that emerges in the market for newspapers "brings supply and demand into equilibrium."[59] The regulatory scheme that the government has adopted for the spectrum does not work in that way. Instead, the government imposes barriers to entry and removes them only for its licensees, to whom it grants the rights for free. After that, the licensee can sell the license at whatever price the market will bear; meanwhile, the licensee will be entitled to all the revenues. When the supply of a revenue-producing asset is artificially limited, and then the asset is given away at a price of zero, there is bound to be "excess demand." But that kind of scarcity is unique to broadcasting only because, with respect to broadcasting but not with respect to print, the government has asserted ownership of an essential factor of production, proceeded to give it away rather than sell it, and prohibited intruders from encroaching.[60]

Finally, broadcasting's unique scarcity may denote the perception that broadcast channels are "peculiarly rare,"[61] in the sense that there are numerically fewer, or comparatively "too few," of them as compared with print outlets. The best answer to that argument resides in three facts: First, the number of available broadcast channels regularly increases. Second, technological advances such as cable TV render broadcast spectrum scarcity as a determinant of the

---

58. *Id.* at 217.

59. *Id.* at 209.

60. Judge Stephen F. Williams refers to that variation of the scarcity rationale as "its generic form (the idea that an excess of demand over supply at a price of zero justifies a unique First Amendment regime)." *Time Warner Entertainment*, 105 F.3d at 724 (Williams, J., dissenting from denial of rehearing *en banc*).

61. *Id.*

number of available broadcast channels obsolete. Third, whereas the number of broadcast channels has actually increased in recent years, the numbers of daily and weekly newspapers has steadily declined.[62] One cannot respond to the "too few" argument with mere numbers or even with comparisons of growth rates of broadcast and print outlets, because the assertion that there are "too few" implies a baseline of "enough." But such a baseline of *enough*, in terms of which we could evaluate the adequacy of what we currently enjoy, does not exist.

The Public Forum as a First Amendment Variation of the Ownership Theme. Analyzing free TV proposals in terms of the public forum doctrine proves to be yet another exercise in conceptual legerdemain. The exercise begins with the assertion of government ownership of the spectrum, which as we have seen is a dubious claim at best. Nevertheless, here as elsewhere it provides a predicate of sorts upon which to build a defense against broadcasters' First Amendment objections to controls in general and free TV requirements in particular. In terms of public forum doctrine, the broadcasters' First Amendment claim in resistance to free TV would be that public ownership of the spectrum does not necessarily imply that the government has blanket authority to regulate the content of what is said over the airwaves. Indeed, the broadcasters might argue that public ownership cuts *against* rather than in favor of content regulation:

> Private and public rights, justified by independent arguments, may often restrict the manner in which the government may use resources that it owns. This argument applies with equal force to the "government-owned" spectrum. Just because the

---

62. KRATTENMAKER & POWE, *supra* note 1, at 216.

government "owns" the spectrum does not mean
that it can control what is said there. Beyond certain "traffic" rules for the airwaves, the First
Amendment may preclude governmental control.
The extent of the First Amendment's control is defined by the public forum doctrines.[63]

Application of the public forum doctrine requires that
the government property in question be classified as either
a *traditional*, a *designated*, or a *nonpublic* forum.[64] If the
property is deemed a *traditional* public forum, such as a
public street or a park that has "time out of mind, . . .
been used for purposes of assembly, communicating
thoughts between citizens, and discussing public questions,"[65] the conventional doctrinal wisdom is that any
regulation of access based on content will be subject to
strict scrutiny and will not pass muster unless it is narrowly
drawn to serve a compelling state interest. A content-
neutral regulation of time, place, and manner of speech
will be sustained if it is narrowly tailored to serve a significant government interest and leaves open alternative channels of communication.[66] If the property is deemed a *designated* public forum, such as is created when the state vol-
untarily chooses to make property available for public
expression, it is—so long as it is available for expression at
all—subject to the same First Amendment standards as a
traditional public forum. In *nonpublic* forums, government
regulation of access and even government regulation of
content are subject to considerably less rigorous scrutiny:
the state may reserve such public assets for their intended
purposes, communicative or otherwise, so long as the

63. Spitzer, *supra* note 47, at 1029.
64. Perry Educ. Ass'n v. Perry Local Educators' Ass'n, 460 U.S. 37
(1983).
65. Hague v. CIO, 307 U.S. 496, 515 (1939).
66. *Perry*, 460 U.S. at 45.

regulation of speech is reasonable and not an effort to suppress expression merely because public officials oppose the speaker's view.[67]

With regard to the constitutionality of free TV, it is possible to spin the public forum categories and their attendant implications so that they point in more than one constitutional direction. According to Professor Matthew L. Spitzer, for example, the kind of controls represented by a free TV requirement might be constitutional on the following reasoning:

> Electromagnetic spectrum, which is neither a street nor a park, is not a traditional public forum. Because the government's system of licensing and content controls predicated thereon precludes any inference of an intent to open the airwaves to all who wish to participate, the electromagnetic spectrum has not been designated a public forum. Therefore, the Court might conclude, the electromagnetic spectrum is only a nonpublic forum, subject to whatever reasonable regulations on speech and access the government wishes to promulgate. Clearly, licensing is a reasonable method of precluding interference, and the content controls that are predicated on licensing are a reasonable adjunct to licensing. They are not only intended to provide an equitable distribution of licenses, but also to guarantee uninterrupted access to the media by the public. Therefore, the existing system of licensing and content controls [and, by extension, the proposed free TV for candidates mandates are] constitutional, as long as broadcasters are not precluded from gaining licenses because of their viewpoints about issues that will be the subject of broadcasts.[68]

---

67. *Id.* at 46.
68. Spitzer, *supra* note 47, at 1038–39. Professor Spitzer confesses

In other words, Professor Spitzer's argument suggests that public forum doctrine might *permit* government to require broadcasters to provide free TV: spectrum is a nonpublic forum owned by government, merely licensed to broadcasters, and government may determine who has access and for what kind of message.

According to Professor William W. Van Alstyne, by contrast, it is possible to argue that the First Amendment might *mandate* "third party rights of access to a broadcast frequency," which is what free TV for candidates would amount to, on the "basis that the frequency is public property and a natural public forum with regard to which the government cannot, constitutionally, discriminate" in favor of licensees.[69] Professor Cass R. Sunstein has endorsed a somewhat similar argument.[70]

Although each may have a superficial credibility, neither of those spins makes a persuasive case that the public forum doctrine offers constitutional support to the free TV proposals. Indeed, neither ultimately persuades that the doctrine is genuinely to the point.[71] But notice how different they are and, accordingly, how the source of their weakness varies. The first theory props up the free TV proposals by what is essentially a prerogative-of-government-ownership argument that puts all First Amend-

---

that the results in the public forum cases "are sufficiently disparate that [he] cannot be certain about how the public forum doctrines might be applied to radio spectrum." *Id.* at 1039 n.291.

69. WILLIAM W. VAN ALSTYNE, FIRST AMENDMENT CASES AND MATERIALS 543 (Foundation Press, 2d ed. 1995).

70. CASS R. SUNSTEIN, DEMOCRACY AND THE PROBLEM OF FREE SPEECH 103 (Free Press 1993).

71. *See* Robert M. O'Neil, *Broadcasting as a Public Forum, in* RATIONALES AND RATIONALIZATIONS: REGULATING THE ELECTRONIC MEDIA 125 (Robert Corn-Revere ed., The Media Institute 1997) (arguing that public forum doctrine is inapt in the broadcasting context and that "licensed broadcast outlets and cable systems cannot properly be classified as public fora for purposes of determining access.").

ment objections to government control—those of broadcasters and of ordinary citizens alike—on the same feeble
footing. That argument founders on the conceptual emptiness of the claim of government spectrum ownership,
which provides illusory cover for what is in reality a naked
assertion of regulatory power.

The second theory props up the free TV proposals by
using the utterly different strategy of implicitly claiming
that free TV is *required* because it would vindicate *citizens'*
First Amendment rights. The theory is a variation on the
Red Lion "rights of listeners and viewers" theme. It is
worth noting that *Red Lion* is the single exception to the
long line of cases unequivocally rejecting its fundamental
premise that the First Amendment is a sword that gives the
government power rather than a shield protecting citizens
from government.[72] In addition, apart from *Red Lion*, the
Court has never itself attempted to put doctrinal flesh on
the bare bones of its assertion of viewers' and listeners'
rights.[73]

Red Lion **Applied.** The scarcity argument upon which
Red Lion was based has been so profoundly discredited—its
conceptual underpinnings so thoroughly undermined, its
empirical premises so utterly annihilated—that it provides
scant support indeed for the current disparity in First
Amendment protection enjoyed by broadcasters and the

---

72. For a discussion, and rejection, of the so-called affirmative theory
of the First Amendment, *see* Lillian R. BeVier, *Money and Politics: A
Perspective on the First Amendment and Campaign Finance Reform*, 73
CALIF. L. REV. 1045 (1985).

73. *Cf.* Lillian R. BeVier, *An Informed Public, An Informing Press:
The Search for a Constitutional Principle*, 68 CALIF. L. REV. 482 (1980)
(arguing that despite the fact that there is a crucial link between constitutionally prescribed processes and the First Amendment, the idea that the
people have an enforceable "right to know" cannot be sustained as a matter of constitutional principle).

print media. Nevertheless, until the Supreme Court explicitly overrules it, one must contend with its doctrinal implications. But even if *Red Lion* itself is still "good law" in the sense that the Court would adhere to its underlying rationale, it does not necessarily confer a constitutional blessing on free TV mandates. The Court has sanctioned two different schemes that more or less *required* certain content to be broadcast. In other cases, it has both permitted the FCC to impose a more onerous ban on broadcast speech than would have been permissible to impose on print media[74] and invalidated a congressionally imposed prohibition of certain broadcaster speech.[75]

Each of the two "required content" schemes is distinguishable in important ways from the free TV mandates. One of them was *Red Lion* itself, in which the Court sustained the fairness doctrine and the personal attack rules. With respect to the fairness doctrine, it is easy to forget how much discretion the broadcasters retained over the way in which—in what format, at what length, and with respect to what issues—they were to fulfill their obligation. Theoretically at least, although fulfilling the obligation might affect their programming decisions somewhat, they retained sufficient control of their program content so that they could minimize their financial losses. With respect to the personal attack rules, while they did require that broadcasters give "free" access to the victims of personal attacks, broadcasters could avoid bringing the obligation into play simply by not engaging in personal attacks. In other words, both the fairness doctrine and the personal attack rules left the broadcaster with significant discretion about

---

74. FCC *v.* Pacifica Foundation, 438 U.S. 726 (1978) (sustaining FCC ban on "indecent" programming). *Pacifica* is not relevant to the present discussion because the rationale for the regulation there at issue was a combination of the need to protect children and captive audiences and the pervasiveness of the broadcast media.

75. FCC *v.* League of Women Voters, 468 U.S. 364 (1984).

how to structure broadcast content. The free TV proposals, by contrast, appear to leave the broadcasters with virtually no discretion about how to fulfill the obligation and no means of escaping it.

The other "required content" case was *CBS, Inc.* v. *FCC.*[76] The Supreme Court there sustained the FCC's reading of section 312(a)(7) of the Communications Act of 1934 to create an affirmative, promptly enforceable right of reasonable access to broadcast stations for individual candidates seeking federal office.[77] The case is far from being controlling authority on the constitutionality of free TV mandates, however, since section 312(a)(7) required broadcasters to *sell* time to candidates, not to give it away as free TV would require. Moreover, even under the rule in *CBS*, broadcasters were left with considerable discretion about how to meet their obligation.

The case that invalidated a congressionally imposed speech prohibition may cut against the free TV mandates' constitutionality under *Red Lion*. In *FCC* v. *League of Women Voters*,[78] the Court rejected section 399 of the Public Broadcasting Act of 1967, which prohibited any noncommercial educational station that received a grant from the Corporation for Public Broadcasting to "engage in editorializing."[79] The Court accepted the government's assertion that section 399 was designed to "safeguard the public's right to a balanced presentation of public issues,"[80] but it was troubled by the fact that the purpose was accomplished by "directly [prohibiting] the broadcaster from

---

76. 453 U.S. 367 (1981).
77. 47 U.S.C. § 312(a)(7).
78. 468 U.S. 364 (1984).
79. 47 U.S.C. § 390 *et seq.*
80. 468 U.S. at 385.

speaking out on public issues."[81] Although the free TV proposals would not share the "direct prohibition" vice,
League of Women Voters suggests that the Court would
strictly scrutinize them despite *Red Lion*—and strict scrutiny is a process that usually proves fatal to challenged
regulations.[82] The likelihood of strict scrutiny stems from
the fact that free TV, like section 399, is "specifically
directed at [expression] that lies at the heart of First
Amendment protection,"[83] so the Court will "be especially
careful in weighing the interests that are asserted [and] in
assessing the precision with which"[84] the regulations are
crafted.

The Same First Amendment Rights for Broadcasters?
League of Women Voters suggests that, even under a constitutional regime in which *Red Lion* is good law, free TV
might have to undergo usually fatal strict scrutiny. What
would be free TV's fate if we assume instead that *Red Lion*
is not good law? The doctrinal issues here are not difficult
to formulate. Even when the analytical path is not obscured
by the scarcity and public ownership smokescreens, however, resolving the issues is no simple task.

One thing is clear: Congress could not compel the print
media to offer a right to reply to candidates similar to the
compelled right of reply imposed on broadcasters and
affirmed in *Red Lion*.[85] In addition, the Court has on many

---

81. *Id.*

82. As Professor Gerald Gunther once observed, scrutiny that is strict
in theory is usually "fatal in fact." Gerald Gunther, *The Supreme Court,
1971 Term—Foreword: In Search of Evolving Doctrine on a Changing
Court: A Model for a Newer Equal Protection*, 86 HARV. L. REV. 1, 8
(1972).

83. 468 U.S. at 381.

84. *Id.* at 382.

85. Miami Herald Publishing Co. *v.* Tornillo, 418 U.S. 241 (1974).

occasions held that private parties may not be required to affirm,[86] distribute,[87] or offer a forum to[88] points of view or beliefs with which they disagree. Those holdings suggest that the Court would look with suspicion on the free TV mandates since they would require broadcasters to give time to candidates whether they agreed with the candidates or not.

On the other hand, the Court in *PruneYard Shopping Center* v. *Robins* has sustained against a First Amendment challenge a state court's reading of a state constitutional provision to prohibit private shopping center owners from denying access to petition circulators.[89] And in *Turner Broadcasting System* v. *FCC (Turner II)*,[90] the Court, albeit narrowly, sustained the "must-carry" provisions of the Cable Television Consumer Protection and Competition Act of 1992 in the face of the cable operators' vigorous First Amendment challenge. *PruneYard* and *Turner II* suggest that the mere fact that free TV would compel broadcasters to carry speech at times not of their own choosing with candidates' expressing views with which the broadcasters might disagree would not necessarily condemn the mandates to First Amendment death. Mandated free TV would, however, condemn them to run a highly nuanced gauntlet of First Amendment questions.

---

86. Wooley *v.* Maynard, 430 U.S. 705 (1977) (state may not punish individuals who cover up the state motto "Live Free or Die" on their license plates); West Virginia State Bd. Educ. *v.* Barnette, 319 U.S. 624 (1943) (compulsory flag salute violates First Amendment).

87. Pacific Gas & Elec. Co. *v.* Public Utils. Comm'n, 475 U.S. 1 (1986) (private utility company may not constitutionally be required to distribute speech of a third party with which it disagrees).

88. Hurley *v.* Irish Am. Gay, Lesbian & Bisexual Group of Boston, 115 S. Ct. 2338 (1995) (private parade organizers may not be required to offer parade space to a group propounding a message with which the organizers disagree).

89. 447 U.S. 74 (1980).

90. 117 S. Ct. 1174 (1997).

Content-Based or Content-Neutral? First is the question of whether the Court would deem free TV to be a control on the *content* of speech. If so, strict scrutiny would ensue, and the mandates would be struck down unless they were finely tuned to serve a compelling state interest—"some pressing public necessity, some essential value that has to be preserved"[91]—with the least restrictive means. On the other hand, if the Court deemed free TV to be content-neutral, the justices would subject it to less demanding review and would sustain it if they thought it "furthers an important or substantial governmental interest; if the governmental interest is unrelated to the suppression of free expression; and if the incidental restriction on alleged First Amendment freedoms is no greater than is essential to the furtherance of that interest."[92]

In one of its more stunning understatements, the Court has acknowledged that "[d]eciding whether a particular regulation is content-based or content-neutral is not always a simple task."[93] Especially is that true when the regulation does not on its face discriminate among viewpoints but instead, like the free TV proposals, proceeds in terms of

---

91. *Turner I*, 512 U.S. at 680 (O'Connor, J., dissenting).
92. United States v. O'Brien, 391 U.S. 367, 377 (1968).
93. *Turner I*, 512 U.S. at 642–43. The Court elaborated:

We have said that the "principal inquiry in determining content-neutrality . . . is whether the government has adopted a regulation of speech because of [agreement or] disagreement with the message it conveys." . . . The purpose, or justification, of a regulation will often be evident on its face . . . . But while a content-based purpose may be sufficient in certain circumstances to show that a regulation is content-based, it is not necessary to such a showing in all cases . . . . Nor will the mere assertion of a content-neutral purpose be enough to save a law which, on its face, discriminates based on content.

Id. (citations omitted).

subject matter, format, or speaker identity.

The Court's decision regarding whether free TV is content-based vis-à-vis the broadcasters will turn in part on the extent to which it regards the mandates as a function of the content of the speech that the *broadcasters* would otherwise utter. In describing the majority's conclusion that must-carry is content-neutral, Justice Anthony Kennedy noted in *Turner I* that the obligation "interfered with cable operators' editorial discretion by compelling them to offer" programming not of their own choosing (and at a considerable loss of revenue). Still, he emphasized, "the extent of the interference does not depend upon the content of the *cable operators'* programming."[94] If that reasoning were to be applied to the free TV mandates, they too would be found content-neutral: they would interfere with broadcasters' editorial discretion and cause them considerable financial pain,[95] but the interference would not be a function of or in any way related to the content of the *broadcasters'* programming.

But the Court's decision regarding whether free TV is content-neutral may not treat as controlling the fact that the required candidate access is not a function of the broadcasters' speech. Instead, what might matter most is that the mandates are speaker-identity, subject-matter, and format-specific. True, the mandates do not single out particular viewpoints for more or less favorable treatment. Apart from the fact that they lack that inevitably fatal flaw, it is hard to imagine regulations that would be less content-neutral: looked at through the lens of what they require of candidates to become entitled to their benefits, they not only prescribe the generic class of qualified speakers (cer-

---

94. *Id.* at 644 (emphasis added).

95. The most common estimate of cost is $500 million per two-year election cycle, an amount that Paul Taylor thinks is "small change to the industry." Taylor, *Fat Cat Broadcasters, supra* note 22, at 2.

tain candidates for federal office) but also dictate the subject matter and the format of the speech. In rejecting strict scrutiny in *Turner I*, the Court noted several significant features of the must-carry obligations that free TV proposals do not share. Must-carry was found to be content-neutral because Congress did not design it "to promote speech of a particular content" nor "as a means of ensuring that particular programs will be shown."[96] The free TV requirements, on the other hand, would ordain the topic and are plainly designed to guarantee that certain kinds of speech will be broadcast. Moreover, in *Turner I* the Court noted with approval in connection with federal funding of noncommercial stations through the Corporation for Public Broadcasting that "the Government is foreclosed from using its financial support to gain leverage over any programming decisions."[97] And it reiterated its long commitment to negating the "risk of an enlargement of government control over the content of broadcast discussion of public issues"[98]—a risk that would materialize in spades should the free TV mandates be implemented.

When the Court said that deciding whether a particular regulation is content-based is "not always . . . simple," it could well have gone on to state the analytic corollary: *predicting* what the Court will decide is an exercise in guesswork, hunch, and intuition every bit as much as it is an exercise in case parsing and straightforward legal analysis.[99] The jurisprudence of content control would give a Court determined to engage in lenient review a plausible if not wholly persuasive rationale for doing so. To me, however, it seems more likely that the Court will find the free

---

96. *Turner I*, 512 U.S. at 649–50.
97. *Id.* at 651.
98. *Id.* at 652 (citation omitted).
99. The best general treatment is Geoffrey R. Stone, *Content-Neutral Restrictions*, 54 U. CHI. L. REV. 46 (1987).

TV mandates content-based, if only as a means of establishing a predicate for strictly scrutinizing them. The free TV mandates would embody such intrusive, particularistic, and overbearing governmental judgments regarding the conduct of political campaigns that the Court will almost certainly insist on a painstaking and skeptical evaluation of the goals they supposedly serve and their aptness as means. And as most Court watchers know, scrutiny that is strict in theory is almost always fatal in fact.

Even if the Court were to determine that the free TV mandates are content-neutral, however, so that they would be given only intermediate scrutiny, they would have a difficult time passing constitutional muster. A regulation's surviving *O'Brien*'s less exacting inquiry into means-ends relationships still requires the Court to be persuaded that the government's interest is important, substantial, and unrelated to the suppression of free expression. In addition,

> [w]hen the Government defends a regulation on speech as a means to redress past harms or prevent anticipated harms, it must do more than simply "posit the existence of the disease sought to be cured." . . . It must demonstrate that the recited harms are real, not merely conjectural, and that the regulation will in fact alleviate these harms in a direct and material way.[100]

Regardless, therefore, of whether the Court applies strict or intermediate scrutiny to the free TV mandates, it will have to discern, articulate, and assess the government's interest; it will have to determine whether the interest is related to the suppression of expression; and it will have to gauge the mandates' effectiveness in terms of the posited goals. I now turn to the analysis of those matters,

---

100. *Turner I*, 512 U.S. at 664 (quoting Quincy Cable TV, Inc. *v.* FCC, 768 F.2d 1434, 1455 (D.C. Cir. 1985)).

all of which—if the Court takes them seriously—bode ill for the constitutional fate of the free TV proposals.[101]

The Government Interest. Supporters have asserted that free TV would accomplish four principal goals. First, by "striking a blow at paid political advertising—the single most expensive part of any political campaign,"[102] free TV would, in the words of President Clinton, "diminish the impact of excessive money" in politics.[103] Second, by fostering a "campaign discourse that favors words over images and substance over sound bites,"[104] free TV would "raise the level of discourse. And it would serve as an

---

101. Note two caveats. First, since proponents of free TV have to date offered no sustained defense of their idea, it is possible that they would characterize or formulate the interests that the mandates supposedly serve differently from the way they have done so far. It is also possible that different formulations of the goals they seek to accomplish would substantially affect the Court's assessment of the state's interest. Thus, what I offer here is an effort to articulate and evaluate free TV's goals as they have until now been enunciated. Should different goals be posited, different evaluations might emerge. Second, since the analysis here is of generic free TV proposals, rather than of any particular species of mandate, my examination of means-end relationships will be less finely grained than were it to focus on a specific plan.

102. Representative Louise Slaughter (D-N.Y.), Press Release on the occasion of her Introduction of H.R. 84: Fairness in Political Advertising Act, which "would require television stations to offer free television time to candidates for statewide or federal office in exchange for renewing or receiving their broadcasting license." Mar. 11, 1997.

103. *Remarks to the Conference on Free TV and Political Reform and an Exchange with Reporters*, 33 WEEKLY COMP. PRES. DOC. 330 (Mar. 11, 1997) [hereinafter *Clinton Remarks on Free TV*].

104. Lawrence O'Rourke, *One Idea to Halt TV Money Rush: Make Ads Free*, SACRAMENTO BEE, May 27, 1997, at A12 (quoting Paul Taylor) ("'Free time would reduce negative advertising. . . . By requiring that candidates talk directly to the camera, free time would raise the level of campaigns. . . . The goal is not to dull the thrust-and-parry of politics but to foster a campaign discourse that favors words over images and substance over sound bites.'").

antidote to the unregulated hit-and-run campaigning of outside groups . . . and the civic corrosion of political attack ads."[105] Third, free TV would "equalize the playing field."[106] And fourth, because "deceptive television ads . . . deepen cynicism and depress turnout,"[107] free TV would, again in the words of President Clinton, restore the "broad confidence of the American people but also of the American press that comments on it."[108]

Whether one characterizes them as trivial or important, vapid or substantial, the first of those four goals is highly problematic in First Amendment terms. It conflicts fundamentally and profoundly with the amendment's core premises. The elaborate and sometimes mystifying doctrinal framework that characterizes First Amendment jurisprudence sometimes tempts regulators to forget that the cases rest on a remarkably solid and unyielding foundation of political freedom.[109] The governing principles celebrate the

---

105. Paul Taylor, *Create a TV Time Bank*, NEW DEMOCRAT, May–June 1997, at 14.

106. Slaughter, *supra* note 102.

107. Paul Taylor, *quoted in* Jacqueline Myers, *Election Over but Not Campaign; Campaign for Free Air Time for Political Candidates*, 85 THE QUILL 10 (Jan. 1997).

108. Clinton, *Remarks on Free TV, supra* note 103.

109. I have previously argued:

The government may not interfere in [citizens'] efforts to persuade their fellow citizens of the merits of particular proposals; nor may it disrupt the free communication of their views, nor penalize them for granting or withholding their support from elected officials on the basis of the positions those officials espouse. Government may neither prescribe an official orthodoxy, require the affirmation of particular beliefs, nor compel citizens to support causes or political activities with which they disagree. Government may neither punish its critics nor impose unnecessary burdens on their political activity. . . . To remain faithful to those principles, one must be vigilant to detect the costs to freedom lurking in reform proposals that come dressed as benign efforts to achieve a

liberty of individuals and private associations to decide for themselves what resources to devote to political activity and abjure the idea that government may regulate, judge, or in any way control the substance or quality of political debate.

Buckley v. *Valeo*[110] is the flagship case that translated those principles into doctrine in the specific context of campaign finance regulation. Not only has *Buckley* not been overruled, but it has stood as a remarkably robust precedent in the seven major campaign finance regulation cases that the Court has decided since.[111] *Buckley* denies government the power to pursue the first goal asserted for free TV. A straight-faced argument that government may regulate campaign activity so as to "diminish the impact of excessive money" in politics would be virtually impossible to maintain in the teeth of the following straightforward Supreme Court pronouncement:

> The First Amendment *denies government the power* to determine that spending to promote one's political views is wasteful, excessive, or unwise. In the free society ordained by our Constitution it is *not the government but the people*—individually as citizens and candidates and collectively as associations and political committees—who must retain control over the quantity and range of debate on public issues in a political campaign.[112]

---

healthy politics.

Lillian R. BeVier, *Campaign Finance "Reform" Proposals: A First Amendment Analysis*, Cato Institute Policy Analysis no. 282, at 22 (Sept. 4, 1997) (footnotes omitted) [hereinafter *Campaign Finance "Reform"*].

110. 424 U.S. 1 (1976).

111. For a description and analysis of the cases, *see* BeVier, *Campaign Finance "Reform," supra* note 109, at 26–29.

112. 424 U.S. at 57 (emphasis added).

No single flagship case crystallizes the First Amendment's hostility to government efforts to "improve the conduct and discourse of politics" or to "combat negative campaigning." Time and again, however, the Court has extolled our "profound national commitment to the principle that debate on public issues should be uninhibited, robust, and wide-open, and that it may well include vehement, caustic and sometimes unpleasantly sharp attacks on government and public officials."[113] While the Court has acknowledged that there is no constitutional value in false statements of fact,[114] it has held that the commitment to uninhibited debate is a virtual trump that substantially limits the ability of public officials to recover damages from defendants who utter false statements about their official performance.[115] Time and again, too, the Court has affirmed that the freedoms protected by the First Amendment are "delicate and vulnerable" and must have adequate "breathing space" to survive.[116] For example, the Court is convinced that trying to protect public discourse from "outrageous" speech would have an "inherent subjectiveness about it which would allow a jury to impose liability on the basis of the jurors' tastes or views, or perhaps on the basis of their dislike of a particular expression."[117] Accordingly, a public official may not recover damages for intentional infliction of emotional distress without showing that the offending publication contains a false statement made in reckless disregard of the truth.[118] And time and again the Court has defended the proposition that "govern-

---

113. New York Times Co. *v.* Sullivan, 376 U.S. 254, 270 (1964).

114. *See, e.g.,* Gertz *v.* Robert Welch, Inc., 418 U.S. 323, 344 (1974).

115. *See, e.g.,* New York Times Co. *v.* Sullivan, 376 U.S. 254 (1964).

116. NAACP *v.* Button, 371 U.S. 415, 433 (1963).

117. Hustler Magazine *v.* Falwell, 485 U.S. 46, 55 (1988).

118. *Id.*

mental bodies may not prescribe the form or content of individual expression":[119]

> The constitutional right of free expression is powerful medicine in a society as diverse and populous as ours. It is designed and intended to remove governmental restraints from the arena of public discussion, putting the decision as to what views shall be voiced largely into the hands of each of us, in the hope that use of such freedom will ultimately produce a more capable citizenry and more perfect polity and in the belief that no other approach would comport with the premise of individual dignity and choice upon which our political system rests.[120]

In light of those often eloquently stated and consistently affirmed First Amendment principles, the second goal sought by proponents of free TV for candidates appears to be out of constitutional bounds. No precedent supports the use of government's coercive power to improve the discourse of politics and combat negative campaigning, whereas the precedents prohibiting pursuit of such a goal are abundant and unwavering.

Buckley v. *Valeo* provides limited guidance on the issue of whether the government may pursue the third goal asserted in behalf of free TV, namely that of "equalizing the playing field." The Court in *Buckley* expressed hostility to equalization efforts: "the concept that government may restrict the speech of some elements in our society in order to enhance the relative voice of others is wholly foreign to

---

119. Cohen *v.* California, 403 U.S. 15, 24 (1971) (reversing the conviction, for disturbing the peace, of a defendant who was observed in the corridor of a municipal court building, wearing a jacket bearing the words "Fuck the Draft").

120. *Id.*

the First Amendment."[121] Providing free TV for all federal candidates does not necessarily fall under that prohibition. Mandating that broadcasters provide free TV time would restrict *their* speech—or at least their editorial discretion— but it would not do so to enhance the relative voice of their *competitors*. It would attempt to equalize the relative voices of candidates vis-à-vis one another, but in doing so it would not restrict any *candidate's* speech.

Under *O'Brien*, though, the goal of "equalizing the playing field" of speech opportunities enjoyed by candidates vis-à-vis one another seems likely to be found to be a goal that is not unrelated to the suppression of free expression, since the need to equalize is a function of differences in communicative impact that would presumably arise absent equalization. A conclusion that such is the case would not necessarily be fatal to the attempt to pursue the goal, but it would dictate that the Court engage in explicitly strict scrutiny.[122]

Only the fourth of the goals that free TV would supposedly accomplish—namely, the goal of restoring the confidence of the American people—seems likely to be unequivocally endorsed by the Court. The Court has never held such a goal to be illegitimate. Indeed, in one case where a similarly formulated goal—that of "preventing diminution of the citizen's confidence in government"[123]—was asserted in defense of a prohibition of corporate campaign speech, the Court called it a goal "of the highest importance."[124] Despite that, the Court determined that the interest was

---

121. *Buckley*, 424 U.S. at 48–49.

122. For a discussion of how a finding that a governmental interest is not unrelated to the suppression of free expression "switches" the Court to a "substantially more demanding" level of scrutiny, *see* John Hart Ely, *Flag Desecration: A Case Study in the Roles of Categorization and Balancing in First Amendment Analysis*, 88 HARV. L. REV. 1482 (1975).

123. First National Bank v. Bellotti, 435 U.S. 765, 787 (1978).

124. *Id.* at 789.

insufficient to sustain the speech regulation there at issue, because no evidence existed to support the government's claim that democratic processes were being undermined by the practices in question.[125]

The Relationship of Means to Ends. Assume *arguendo* an unlikely proposition, namely, that the Court would find all four of free TV's posited goals to be important and constitutionally legitimate. The next task for proponents would be to demonstrate that the goals are real, not merely conjectural or rhetorical, and that free TV would achieve them in a direct and immediate way. Here, unless they are able to come up with more substantial evidence than they have produced to date, the proponents are likely to founder. Indeed, it is as apt to note of the free TV proposals as of the recent spate of campaign finance regulations that they are neither

> premised on empirical analysis, nor derived from established postulates, nor defended in terms of predictions about testable results. Rather [they] rest on pejorative and highly charged rhetoric, [are] formulated in ill-defined but evocative terms, and . . . defended with extravagant claims about benign effects. Yet upon analysis, the picture the [free TV proponents] paint—both of political reality and of the goals of reform—is so vague that it begs all the important questions.[126]

Merely posing some of the questions that the free TV proposals beg makes the analytical point. First, even assuming that reforming "skyrocketing costs of running" for office is a legitimate legislative project, how could giving federal candidates free TV time keep overall costs down?

---

125. *Id.*
126. BeVier, *Campaign Finance "Reform," supra* note 109, at 24.

Since any effort actually to *prohibit* candidates from continuing to spend on their campaigns would run into an impenetrable constitutional barrier,[127] what besides wishful thinking would prevent candidates from using the money saved by free TV to engage in other expensive campaign maneuvers?

Second, again confronted by the impenetrable constitutional barrier to candidate spending limits, so that candidates with access to more resources could continue to spend more even after accepting free TV, how would providing free TV to less well-financed candidates "equalize the playing field"? Even if proponents somehow found a way to equalize the total spending of candidates accepting free TV, how would the incumbent's already considerable advantage be "equalized" away?

Third, given that direct regulations of, or prohibitions regarding, the content and quality of political discourse are placed beyond legislative power by the First Amendment, how would merely providing free TV time to candidates "foster a campaign discourse that favors words over images and substance over sound bites"?

Fourth, what evidence exists that citizens were actually and to their detriment *misled* by what proponents of free TV claim were "deceptive" ads in the 1996 campaign or at other times? And even if citizens were, why is it not enough that the candidates are free to engage in counter speech? (Do we really want the government to monitor the truthfulness of campaign speech, to begin canvassing past campaign speech and voters' reaction to it, to determine whether all the claims were true and, if not, whether citizens were misled by false claims? The implications of such an inquiry are truly devastating to the idea of a "self-governing" people.) Moreover, if citizens have recently become more cynical about politics and have lost some of

---

127. *Buckley*, 424 U.S. at 82.

their confidence in government, what evidence supports the claim that such a phenomenon is accounted for by the way politicians *campaign* rather than by the way they *behave when in office?*

Finally, upon what evidence do advocates of free TV think that "there is a real hunger for political information,"[128] and what makes them think that free TV would satisfy that appetite? Upon what evidence do they conclude that citizens hungry for political information cannot find plenty to satisfy them from the rich and varied menu now provided by the free—that is, genuinely *un*regulated—political debate?

If the Court takes at all seriously its obligation to call what appears on the present state of the evidence to be a rhetorical bluff of free TV's proponents—if it truly requires them to "demonstrate that the recited harms are real, not merely conjectural, and that the regulation will in fact alleviate these harms in a direct and material way"[129]—the proponents will have to come up with well-founded answers to the kinds of questions posed above. They will, in other words, have to offer a defense much more solid than the vague generalities and unsupported assertions about causes and effects that they have offered so far.

The First Amendment Rights of Candidates. The implicitly skeptical empirical premise of the foregoing rhetorical questions is that, unless it is bolstered by significant additional constraints, free TV alone will do little to accomplish its proponents' highly touted goals. Accordingly, the proposals contemplate regulating the speech of candidates who accept free TV by exacting some kind of quid pro quo from them: candidates must agree to appear in person, to

---

128. James Bennett, *Perils of Free Air Time,* N.Y. TIMES, Mar. 13, 1997, at A1 (quoting Paul Taylor).

129. *Turner I,* 512 U.S. at 664.

face the camera, to talk for a specified length of time, or to accept limits on overall campaign spending, or they must agree to all of those conditions. Restrictions like those—on the quality, quantity, content, or format of political campaign speech—would surely not be tolerated if Congress or the FCC attempted to impose them as free-standing rules.[130] Proponents of free TV may think that the restrictions will enjoy a different constitutional fate if they are defended as reasonable conditions on candidates' receipt of governmentally provided subsidies. But proponents would be mistaken.

Proponents would begin their defense of the conditions by analogizing them to provisions implicitly endorsed by the Court in *Buckley*, when it qualified its otherwise unequivocal rejection of expenditure limitations:

> Congress may engage in public funding of election campaigns and may condition acceptance of public funds on an agreement by the candidate to abide by specified expenditure limitations. Just as a candidate may voluntarily limit the size of the contributions he chooses to accept, he may decide to forgo private fundraising and accept public funding.[131]

Proponents of free TV would also cite *Rust* v. *Sullivan*,[132] in which the Court sustained against First Amendment challenge a Department of Health and Human Services "gag rule" that prohibited recipients of federal family planning funds from providing abortion information. The Court held that the gag rule was a permissible means of safeguarding the integrity of the government program for which taxpayer funds were being expended.[133]

---

130. *See* text accompanying notes 97–105, *supra*.
131. *Buckley*, 424 U.S. at 57 n.65.
132. 500 U.S. 173 (1991).
133. *Rust*, 500 U.S. at 196 ("the Government is simply insisting that

Proponents of free TV would reason that because candidates would receive free TV time, *Buckley* and *Rust* would support the imposition on them of quality, content, or format restrictions to achieve the purposes of the government program. But neither *Rust* nor *Buckley* would support them because the key fact in both cases was that the subsidy was supplied *by the taxpayers*. The key fact about free TV, on the other hand, is that the subsidy would be provided *by the broadcasters*.

Indeed, analysis of free TV in terms of *Buckley* and *Rust* exposes the proposals for the constitutional shell game that they are. Broadcasters would have no First Amendment rights to resist compliance with the free TV mandates, proponents say, because spectrum scarcity or some variation of the public ownership trope permits government to regulate licensees' speech in the public interest; they would have no Fifth Amendment right to compensation because the "property" to be taken does not "belong" to them; and candidates would have no First Amendment right to resist compliance with the format, quality, or content controls, because they would be permitted to speak for free. It does not require X-ray vision to detect the conceptual emptiness of that series of tricky doctrinal maneuvers. The First Amendment edifice of political freedom that the Court has so painstakingly constructed seems unlikely to yield to such transparently feeble arguments on behalf of overbearing government control.

The Proposals Assessed

The basic idea of free TV for political candidates lacks a constitutional foundation. Nor can it be justified in policy terms. Those conclusions do not fundamentally change depending on which particular proposal one considers: the

---

public funds be spent for the purposes for which they were authorized").

constitutional devil in those proposals lurks in their very conception, while the policy devil lurks in the mismatch of ends and means that inevitably follows when policymakers attempt to give real-world shape to basically ill-conceived notions. Since that is the case, quibbling over regulatory detail at this stage of the debate would be unproductive. Thus, this monograph does not undertake either to describe or to examine the particulars of any of the proposals. Indeed, President Clinton's call for free TV for political candidates in his 1998 State of the Union address, and the surfacing of such a proposal by FCC Chairman William Kennard immediately thereafter, suggest that the details of perhaps the most prominent proposals have yet to be determined.[134]

The Proposals. To enhance appreciation of the constitutional and policy issues that they raise, I briefly summarize the most prominently touted of the plans—two that have been introduced in Congress and one that has been advocated by a private group.

The McCain-Feingold Bill. One version of the McCain-Feingold Bipartisan Campaign Reform Act of 1997, S. 25, included a free TV time provision. It would have amended section 315 of the Communications Act of 1934,[135] the "equal time for candidates" provision, to require broadcasting stations within a candidate's state or an adjacent state to provide "eligible" Senate candidates with thirty minutes of free prime broadcast time.[136] To become "eligible" for the time, Senate candidates would have had

---

134. Lawrie Mifflin, *State of the Union: Political Broadcasts; F.C.C. Plans to Take Look at Free Political Broadcasts*, N.Y. TIMES, Jan. 29, 1998, at A19.

135. 47 U.S.C. § 315.

136. S. 25, 105th Cong., 2d Sess. § 102 (1997).

to agree to abide by campaign spending limits and to limit their acceptance of contributions from out-of-state donors.[137] No single station would have had to provide more than fifteen minutes of free time; and candidates would have been required to use the time in segments of not less than thirty seconds or more than five minutes.[138] Within a certain prescribed time before an election, the bill would in addition have required stations to sell broadcast time to eligible candidates at 50 percent of the station's "lowest charge . . . for the same amount of time for the same period on the same date."[139]

The Slaughter Bill. In March 1997 Representative Louise Slaughter, a Democrat from New York, introduced H.R. 84, the Fairness in Political Advertising Act. In exchange for receiving or renewing a broadcast license, the act would have required broadcasters to offer free TV time to candidates for statewide or federal office.[140] Stations would have been required to offer an equal amount of free time per candidate, but not less than a total of two hours and in units of not more than five minutes and not less than ten seconds. No broadcaster would have been required to provide more than four and a half hours per week. Candidates would have been required to speak directly into the camera.[141]

Free TV for Straight Talk Coalition. The privately organized Free TV for Straight Talk Coalition, founded by former *Washington Post* reporter Paul Taylor, has joined with a group of scholars—Norman J. Ornstein of the

---

137. *Id.* at § 503.
138. *Id.* at § 502.
139. *Id.* at § 103.
140. H.R. 84, 105th Cong., 2d Sess. § 2(a) (1997).
141. *Id.* at § 2(c).

American Enterprise Institute, Thomas E. Mann of the Brookings Institution, Michael J. Malbin of the State University of New York at Albany, and Anthony Corrado, Jr., of Colby College—in endorsing the creation of a "broadcast bank." Although the "broadcast bank" proposal has taken a number of slightly different forms, its broad outlines have remained essentially as follows. Every radio and TV station in the country would be required to contribute at least two hours of prime spot time each two-year election cycle. The contributions would be deposited into a broadcast bank. They would be assigned a monetary value based on market rates where they originated, and the bank would distribute vouchers denominated in money to the Federal Election Commission, which would in turn dispense them. Half the value of the vouchers would go directly to House and Senate candidates who qualified for them by raising over a threshold amount in small contributions from their own districts or states, and the other half would go to the parties, which could distribute the vouchers as they deemed most prudent, given their electoral prospects and the relative strengths and weaknesses of their slates of candidates. Candidates and parties could use the vouchers at any stations they wished, but no message could be less than sixty seconds long. The candidate would be required to appear on screen for the duration of the TV message, and the candidate's voice would be required for radio messages. At the end of every election cycle, the bank would reimburse stations that redeemed more than two hours' worth of free time with proceeds that it would collect from stations that redeemed less. Candidates wishing to purchase time outside the broadcast bank system would be free to do so, but at full market rates: the existing requirement that broadcasters charge political candidates the lowest unit rate for paid political advertising would be repealed.[142]

---

142. *New Campaign Finance Reform Proposals for the 105th Con-*

The Assessment. For the reasons detailed earlier, all the free TV proposals are constitutionally vulnerable. A brief recapitulation of why that is so will serve to emphasize the point.

In Fifth Amendment terms, the proposals push the government ownership claim to the breaking point. On the most rudimentary functional economic analysis of how the licensing system actually works and is administered, the free TV mandates would constitute a taking of property. By requiring that broadcasters forgo substantial income from the sale of broadcast time during the license period, or by assessing broadcasters a "fee" derived solely from their sales of political ads and devoting it solely to funding candidate time, each of the free TV proposals not only would constitute an obviously coercive wealth transfer but also would unacceptably disrupt the broadcasters' legitimate, government-induced, investment-backed expectations.

In First Amendment terms, and looking initially at their impact on broadcasters' rights, the proposals all raise serious concerns even if the Court continues to adhere to *Red Lion*'s broadly discredited scarcity fiction. That is so because each of the post–*Red Lion* cases in which the Court gave its blessing to government-imposed content requirements is distinguishable in fundamentally important ways from the free TV mandates. If the Court were to play one or another of the variations on the ownership theme to analyze the broadcasters' First Amendment rights, the

---

gress (issued Dec. 17, 1996; revised May 7, 1997); Reforming Campaign Finance, BROOKINGS HOME PAGE, http://www.brookings.org/gs/newcfr/reform.htm. One version of the broadcast bank plan plays a variation on that theme. It would finance the plan by an explicit trade-off, repealing the lowest unit rate requirement and in return assessing each broadcaster a fee, payable in "dollars or minutes," on all political advertising the broadcaster sells, with revenues going to the broadcast bank. Norman J. Ornstein, *Forget Sweeping Reform: Here Are 5 Realistic Changes*, ROLL CALL, Jan. 9, 1997, at 34.

result might be somewhat more in doubt, but only because a Court willing to take the spurious ownership claims seriously would thereby signal its willingness to ignore basic First Amendment principles. If the Court, on the other hand, were to abandon *Red Lion*, reject the owner- ship metaphor, and analyze the free TV mandates as though broadcasters enjoyed the same First Amendment rights as members of the print media, the mandates would almost surely succumb to the broadcasters' First Amend- ment challenge. Among other causes for constitutional skepticism is the fact that the governmental interests that free TV would supposedly advance are either impermissible or ill-served by the scheme.

In addition, all the proposals would, in one way or another, violate candidates' First Amendment rights. McCain-Feingold would do so by impermissibly and with- out adequate justification requiring candidates to sacrifice their right to spend their own resources to advocate their own election; it would also unjustifiably dictate the format of candidate speech. Both the fairness in political adver- tising proposal and the broadcast bank proposal would do so by dictating in even more intrusive and impermissible detail the format of candidate speech. The broadcast bank proposal, in addition, would condition candidates' receipt of vouchers on their raising certain kinds of contributions from in-state supporters. The condition has no apparent connection to the "reduce the cost of campaigning" and "make political discourse more substantive" goals that the proposal is touted as serving.

Its proponents often portray free TV as something of a panacea—a practically painless cure for practically all of our campaign-financing woes. They should be more skepti- cal about the idea that they have so enthusiastically em- braced. In all its incarnations it is almost certainly uncon- stitutional. For any embodiment of it to pass constitutional muster, the Court would have to suspend quite completely its usual disbelief with regard to regulations that govern political speech. In addition, it would have to permit itself to become the victim of a constitutional shell game. While the arguments on behalf of free TV may permit doctrinal *i*s to *appear* to be dotted and the *t*s to be crossed, closer analysis shows that they misconceive the fundamental premises of both the First and the Fifth Amendments.

In policy terms, too, free TV has serious weaknesses. First, the goals it claims to pursue are impermissible objectives for a government in a free society. Second, it is unlikely that free TV would in fact come anywhere close to achieving its posited objectives. Third, "free" TV is not free; neither does it represent—as its supporters try to imply—a *public* subsidy provided by *public* funds. Instead, it represents a subsidy provided by *broadcasters*.

Those three weaknesses might be enough to condemn the idea to oblivion, but there is a fourth: no matter what scheme of free TV were to be adopted, implementing the free TV mandates would be an administrative nightmare. All the free TV proposals and all the optimistic urgings on their behalf by their supporters imply through silence about administrative details that free TV would be practically self-executing. Proponents insinuate that getting the time slots in equitable portions *from* the broadcasters, allocating them *to* the appropriate federal candidates, and then making arrangements so that the eligible candidates actually get *on the air with the required format and the suitably crafted message in the relevant market* are simple tasks, easily accomplished merely by ordering them to be done.

Proponents of free TV also imply that enforcement would be without cost or complexity, whether the task be assigned to the Federal Election Commission or to the FCC. The truth is completely otherwise, however, as a moment's reflection will reveal. Consider the range of quid pro quos that the mandates contemplate, multiply them by the number of candidates for federal office, and you will have a sense of the sheer number of enforcement issues that might arise. Divide the number of hours of free time, again by the number of federal candidates deemed eligible to receive the benefit, and you will discern a second layer of complexity. Understand that all those enforcement tasks will be assigned to government officials and think carefully about the intensity of monitoring that ensuring compliance will require. You will understand and quite likely share the fear of its freedom-loving opponents that "free TV" will inevitably entail a very significant expansion of government intrusion into and control of core political activity.

Conclusion

The claims of free TV's supporters obscure each of the policy weaknesses. That is a somewhat surprising fact, given the concern they so often express about misleading campaign ads and the quality of campaign discourse. As the debate on free TV progresses, however—whether it takes place in legislative chambers or in courts or in the hearings of administrative bodies—the idea's proponents have an obligation to drop some of their rhetorical camouflage and forthrightly to address those very significant substantive issues.

In addition, the severity of the constitutional concerns that the free TV proposals raise should worry not just lawyers and judges, nor should only potential opponents of the proposals address them. The constitutional analysis should disconcert proponents of free TV too, because the constitutional problems do not merely represent artifacts of dry and lifeless legal doctrines. To the contrary, the problems arise because the proposals themselves are to a disturbing extent inconsistent with traditions and values that many if not most Americans revere deeply, despite whatever misgivings they may have about negative campaigning and the costs of running for political office.

Political freedom and a collective unwillingness to cast the burdens of public improvements on the few rather than the many are traits that have characterized American democracy since the founding of the Republic. The free TV proposals would put both traits at grave risk.

About the Author

LILLIAN R. BEVIER is the Doherty Charitable Foundation Professor and the Class of 1948 Professor of Scholarly Research at the University of Virginia Law School. On the faculty at the University of Virginia Law School since 1973, she teaches property, intellectual property, and constitutional law, with a specialization in the First Amendment. Professor BeVier has published widely on intellectual property and First Amendment issues in such journals as the *California Law Review*, the *Columbia University Law Review*, the *Harvard Journal of Law and Public Policy*, the *Journal of Law and Economics*, the *Supreme Court Review*, and the *University of Chicago Law Review*.

Professor BeVier graduated from Smith College in 1961 and Stanford Law School in 1965.